Original title:
Crafting Spaces

Copyright © 2024 Creative Arts Management OÜ
All rights reserved.

Author: Tim Wood
ISBN HARDBACK: 978-9916-88-082-1
ISBN PAPERBACK: 978-9916-88-083-8

The Geometry of Serenity

In quiet shapes, the silence grows,
Angles meet where stillness flows.
Circles whisper tales of peace,
In the heart, unease must cease.

Lines connect in soft embrace,
Every curve finds its own place.
Symmetry in twilight's glow,
Within the mind, calm rivers flow.

Layers of Life's Canvas

Brushstrokes dance in vibrant hue,
Tales of old and dreams anew.
Each layer tells a story grand,
Crafted gently by time's hand.

Textures blend, emotions rise,
Beneath the paint, the spirit lies.
Every color, every line,
Intertwined, our hearts align.

Reflections in Still Waters

Glassy surface, calm and deep,
Secrets hidden, buried sleep.
Mirrored skies and drifting leaves,
Nature's breath, the heart believes.

Ripples dance with whispered grace,
Time and space find their place.
In the depths, we search and find,
What the soul has left behind.

Boundaries of Belonging

Lines are drawn, yet hearts expand,
In the shadows, we make our stand.
Together found, yet apart we feel,
A tapestry of wounds to heal.

Each story shared, a bridge anew,
In every glance, a world to view.
Boundaries fade when love ignites,
In the daylight, unity unites.

Nesting the Heart

In the quiet dusk, shadows play,
A tender whisper, night meets day.
Feathers gather, soft and light,
Cradling dreams, in the gentle night.

Hopes entwined like branches strong,
In this space, we all belong.
Love's embrace, a woven art,
Finding comfort, nesting the heart.

Chambers of Recovery

In the silence, echoes call,
Deep within the healing wall.
Tears like rivers, flowing free,
In these chambers, I find me.

Time unfolds like petals bright,
Guiding shadows into light.
Mending pieces, soft repair,
In the silence, we still care.

The Language of Layout

Lines and curves in harmony,
Sketching dreams for all to see.
Colors speak in vibrant tones,
Mapping hearts, we aren't alone.

Textures blend like voices true,
Every choice, a part of you.
Crafting worlds with thought and grace,
The language spoken finds its place.

Sanctuaries Beneath the Surface

Beneath the waves, a world concealed,
Secrets kept, the heart revealed.
Coral castles, deep and grand,
In this sanctuary, we take a stand.

Echoes of the ocean's song,
A sacred space where we belong.
Finding peace in depths so wide,
Sanctuaries that we can't hide.

Heritage of Haven

In the whispers of the past,
Roots intertwine and last,
Stories etched in bark and stone,
A bond that calls us home.

Faded photographs in frames,
Echoes of forgotten names,
Time's embrace in gentle sway,
Guides us through each passing day.

The Comfort of Corners

In cozy nooks where shadows play,
Softened light at end of day,
Books and blankets, laughter's cheer,
Here we find what we hold dear.

Walls that cradle dreams untold,
Whispers in the heart as gold,
The warmth of tea, a hug's delight,
Wrapped in peace, we anchor tight.

Spaces That Breach Silence

A gentle breeze through open doors,
Carries secrets from the shores,
Voices dance in twilight's grace,
Filling voids, a shared embrace.

In moments hushed, the world feels wide,
Timeless truths we cannot hide,
Every breath a chance to start,
Uniting souls, heart to heart.

Portraits of the Present

In every smile, a story spun,
A canvas bright, where life is fun,
Each moment, a brush stroke bold,
Tales of warmth and laughter told.

Vivid hues of day unfold,
In echoes strong, we are consoled,
Living art, we paint our days,
With every breath, in endless ways.

Havens of Light

In the morn, a gentle glow,
Whispers of hope, soft and slow.
Through the cracks, the sun will peek,
Finding warmth in light we seek.

Golden rays on paths we tread,
Leading dreams where hearts are led.
Every shadow finds its place,
In these havens, find your grace.

Palette of Possibilities

Brush in hand, colors collide,
Mixing dreams that flow inside.
Bright and bold, new worlds await,
Each stroke opens up the gate.

Canvas wide, imagination's flight,
Crafting visions, pure delight.
Every hue tells a story,
In this palette, find your glory.

Threads of Boundless Imagination

Weaving dreams through night's embrace,
Stitch by stitch, we find our place.
A tapestry of hopes so grand,
In every thread, a guiding hand.

Colors weave and patterns flow,
Stories rich begin to glow.
In the fabric, futures bloom,
From the loom, dispel the gloom.

Shelters of Solitude

In whispers soft, the quiet calls,
Within four walls, our heart enthralls.
Silence wraps like a gentle shawl,
Here in solitude, we stand tall.

Thoughts like clouds drift in the air,
Finding peace with time to spare.
In the stillness, truths unfold,
Shelters of solitude, pure gold.

Hollowed Hearts of Wood

In the forest deep and wide,
Trees stand tall, their stories hide.
Hollowed hearts that time has carved,
Whispers of the past preserved.

Branches bare, yet strong they stand,
Roots entwined in earthy band.
Nature's grace, both wild and free,
Hollowed hearts, where dreams will be.

The Essence of Embrace

In the warmth of evening light,
Two souls dance, hearts taking flight.
Hands entwined, a gentle squeeze,
The essence found in moments seized.

Eyes that sparkle, soft and bright,
In silence, they share the night.
Whispers low, a tender sigh,
The essence of love fills the sky.

Labyrinth of Layers

Hidden paths beneath the skin,
Layers deep, where dreams begin.
Every turn, a tale unfolds,
Labyrinth where fate beholds.

Truth and shadows intertwine,
Navigating what's divine.
In the heart, the secrets lie,
Labyrinth of layers, we it ply.

Sculpted Stillness

In a garden, soft and green,
Silence reigns, serenity seen.
Every leaf a work of art,
Sculpted stillness, calm impart.

Gentle breezes whoosh and play,
Whispers of the night and day.
In this peace, we find reprieve,
Sculpted stillness, hearts believe.

Creating Cohesion in Chaos

In a world of swirling streams,
We find bonds in tangled dreams.
Amid the noise, we plant a seed,
To grow the unity we need.

Voices clash like iron and glass,
Yet in discord, calm can amass.
Together we weave, hand in hand,
From chaos, a symphony planned.

Echoes fade to softened sighs,
Connection blooms under vast skies.
By joining hearts, we pave the way,
To light the dark and guide the day.

In every storm, a spark can gleam,
Creating order from a shared dream.
Through trials, together we stand,
Finding strength in the chaos, so grand.

Picturesque Pockets of Calm

In the midst of a bustling street,
A quiet corner offers retreat.
Soft whispers of the evening breeze,
Invite the heart to find its ease.

Sunset paints the sky with grace,
A tranquil moment, this cherished space.
Leaves dance gently in lullaby,
While twilight wraps the world in sighs.

Beneath the sky's celestial dome,
We find a stillness, a place called home.
In gardens where the shadows play,
Our worries melt, they drift away.

These pockets in time, a sacred find,
A moment of peace for heart and mind.
Within the chaos, calm remains,
A refuge in life's wild terrains.

Harmonies of Habitat

In the forest, whispers may sing,
A chorus where all creatures cling.
Beneath the boughs, life intertwines,
A dance of rhythms, nature's lines.

Rivers flow with a gentle sway,
Each drop part of the grand ballet.
Mountains echo the calls of old,
Stories of habitats unfold.

Colors burst in the morning light,
In harmony, they take their flight.
The buzzing bees, the rustling trees,
Create a song carried by the breeze.

Earth's symphony, rich and profound,
In every heartbeat, life is found.
Together we thrive, in love and grace,
In every nook, our shared space.

Secrets of Safe Spaces

Amid the hustle, there lies a door,
To realms where worries are no more.
With every sigh, the weight will lift,
In safe spaces, we find our gift.

The warmth of laughter, a gentle touch,
In shared silence, we heal so much.
Walls of trust that softly surround,
In every heartbeat, peace is found.

Here, secrets bloom beneath the stars,
In the comfort of open hearts.
With whispered hopes, we build anew,
In the safety of me and you.

So let us gather, unmask our fears,
In these spaces, we dry our tears.
Within the circle, love will trace,
The hidden beauty of this safe place.

Silence Wrapped in Warmth

In the stillness, hearts connect,
Whispers linger, soft and sweet.
Reassurance in every breath,
A gentle touch, a quiet heat.

In the twilight, shadows fade,
Comfort found in silent grace.
Wrapped in layers, warmth cascades,
Time slows down, a cherished space.

Echoes dance in golden light,
Holding dreams from dusk till dawn.
In the hush, the world feels right,
A tender bond that lingers on.

Beyond the noise, we find our song,
In silence, love can truly thrive.
Wrapped in warmth, we both belong,
Together, simply, we arrive.

Shapes of Solace

In the quiet, forms unfold,
Curves of comfort, lines divine.
Angles where our fears grow cold,
Structures built on love's design.

Glimmers of hope in shadows cast,
Spaces where our hearts can heal.
Every moment, made to last,
In the shapes, our truths reveal.

Patterns woven, intertwined,
Creating solace in our midst.
In the stillness, hearts aligned,
Each breath shared, a gentle tryst.

Echoing in soft refrain,
Every shape a story told.
In this space, we feel no pain,
Finding warmth in shapes of gold.

Rooms of Resonance

Within these walls, we softly tread,
Each corner holds a cherished sound.
Moments linger, gently spread,
In every room, our love is found.

Whispers echo in the air,
Resonance of hearts entwined.
A tranquil space, free from care,
In these rooms, we seek and find.

Windows open to the light,
Sunbeams dance upon the floor.
In this haven, pure delight,
Together, we explore once more.

Memories painted on the walls,
Laughter lingers, sweet and clear.
In these rooms, our spirit calls,
Holding close all we hold dear.

The Bliss of Being

In a moment, we embrace,
Time suspended, hearts aligned.
Finding joy in this warm space,
A simple truth, love is blind.

Breathing deep, we share the air,
In the now, there's pure release.
Awareness blooms in tender care,
The bliss of being, sweet peace.

Hands entwined, we close our eyes,
Lost in dreams that gently flow.
Underneath the vast, wide skies,
The bliss we hold begins to grow.

Every heartbeat, every sigh,
Crafting memories to hold tight.
In this bliss, we learn to fly,
Together, basking in the light.

Inhabitancy of Imagination

In the corners of my mind,
Where dreams take flight and twist,
Colors dance in vibrant hues,
Inhabitancy of bliss.

Echoes whisper in the night,
Stories crafted, deep and wide,
A world where thoughts ignite,
And secrets dare to hide.

Mountains made of paper dreams,
Rivers flow with words unsaid,
Every thought, a thread that gleams,
In this place, we tread.

Each shadow holds a tale untold,
In this realm, we freely roam,
Imagination's spark, so bold,
Forever is our home.

A Symphony of Spaces

A canvas stretched with breaths of air,
Where echoes play and whispers chime,
A symphony in silent layers,
Each note, a heartbeat, keeps the time.

Rooms alive with shadows' sway,
Walls that hold the laughter's trace,
Moments weave in soft ballet,
In every line, a sacred place.

Light cascades on polished floors,
Colors mingle, swirling bright,
Each corner sings of love's outdoors,
A warmth that wraps like soft daylight.

Harmony in every breath,
Where space and soul entwine as one,
In symphony, we find our depth,
As day slips softly into sun.

Mutual Embrace of Room and Heart

In chambers where our laughter flows,
Walls cradle memories shared and pure,
A tender space where kindness grows,
Mutual embrace, our hearts endure.

Beneath the arch of silent beams,
Every glance, a gentle tie,
Together weaving fragile dreams,
In this refuge, we can fly.

The air is thick with unspoken trust,
A shelter warmed by love's soft glow,
Within these walls, we find what's just,
In every shadow, a story's flow.

Room and heart in sweet accord,
A sanctuary built on care,
In this bond, we're gently moored,
Forever free within our lair.

Sanctuaries of the Mind

Within the labyrinth of thought,
Sanctuaries built from dreams,
Each echo holds the lessons taught,
In silent peace, the spirit gleams.

Oh, wandering through memories vast,
Reflections dance on whispered streams,
We seek a place where shadows cast,
Illuminate the hidden themes.

Thoughts entwine like vines in bloom,
Roots that anchor, yet expand,
In this haven, dispel the gloom,
Together, we will boldly stand.

Sanctuaries of the mind,
Where troubles fade and hopes take flight,
In every corner, we will find,
The joy that lives in endless light.

Harbor for the Soul

In the quiet dusk, time slows,
Waves whisper secrets that nobody knows.
Sheltered shores cradle weary dreams,
In the harbor's light, hope gently beams.

Anchored hearts find solace near,
With every tide, we shed our fear.
Stars reflect on tranquil seas,
The soul finds peace in whispered pleas.

Gentle winds carry tales untold,
Embracing warmth, when nights grow cold.
In stillness, we discover our role,
For every heart, a harbor for the soul.

Moonlight dances on darkened waves,
Ebbing sorrows, the soul it saves.
As the night wraps around, we see,
In this sanctuary, we are free.

Corners Cradling Memories

In dusty corners, shadows loom,
Echoes of laughter fill the room.
Memories linger in fleeting light,
Guarded secrets of day and night.

Old photographs, tales untold,
Faded faces, warm and bold.
Every frame holds time in a grip,
Remnants of joy on a nostalgic trip.

Windows frame the passing years,
Carrying both laughter and tears.
In each cranny, stories arise,
A tapestry woven with love's ties.

With whispered whispers, they call to me,
In corners where memories long to be.
As time flows on, I cherish each glance,
A dance with the past in life's sweet trance.

An Atlas of Atmospheres

In every breeze, a story breathes,
Colors painted in autumn leaves.
Mountains echo with ancient chants,
In valleys where the wildflower plants.

Skyward, the stars write their tales,
Guiding lost ships with gentle gales.
Clouds drift softly like whispered dreams,
Time flows slowly in moonlit streams.

Each sunrise brings a vibrant hue,
Awakening earth with the morning dew.
Sunsets blend in a fiery embrace,
Nature's palette, a mystical space.

From deserts wide to oceans deep,
An atlas of atmospheres we keep.
In each locale, a heartbeat flows,
Life's intricate tapestry glows.

Construction of Calm

In the chaos, I seek my peace,
Building walls where worries cease.
With every breath, I lay a stone,
A sanctuary, a space my own.

Gentle rain taps on the ground,
Nature's rhythm, a soothing sound.
Branches sway in a tender dance,
In this stillness, I find my chance.

Soft whispers of the evening breeze,
Carry away my fears with ease.
In the twilight, I close my eyes,
Constructing calm beneath the skies.

Every moment, a brick well-placed,
In the quiet, my heart's embraced.
Here in the silence, I've found my way,
A construction of calm in the fray.

Caresses of Creation

Soft whispers in the dawn,
Brush of light on waking trees.
Each petal holds a gentle yawn,
Nature breathes in tranquil ease.

Colors burst in vibrant play,
Laughter dances in the breeze.
Forming worlds in bright array,
Crafting dreams with tender keys.

Every stone, a tale to tell,
In the earth, the magic flows.
Mysteries that weave and swell,
In the heart, the wonder grows.

Let the spirit roam unfurled,
In the garden of the mind.
Caresses of the unseen world,
In creation, solace find.

Mosaic of Moments

Each heartbeat a glimmer bright,
Fragments of laughter intertwine.
Memories take their sacred flight,
In shadows where the heart does shine.

Caught in fleeting, tender glances,
Time bends softly, sweetly spins.
Life's rhythm in a thousand dances,
In every loss, a new hope begins.

Stitched in threads of joy and pain,
Moments blossom, fade, and grow.
A tapestry, love's sweet refrain,
In the fabric of life, we flow.

Every day a piece to find,
In the mosaic, we belong.
In the whispers of the mind,
Together, we create our song.

Tides of Tranquility

Waves that kiss the sandy shore,
Softly calming, ever near.
Each ebb and flow, a quiet lore,
Whispers only the heart can hear.

Moonlit dances on the sea,
Stars reflected, dreams take flight.
In the night, we find the key,
To unlock peace with gentle light.

Crickets sing their nighttime hymn,
Nature's breath, a soothing balm.
In the darkness, shadows swim,
Wrapped in twilight's tender calm.

Hold the moment, breathe it in,
Let the pulse of life embrace.
Tides will soften where we've been,
In tranquility, find our place.

Edges of Enchantment

In the twilight's vivid hues,
Secrets dance in whispered air.
Magic glimmers, silent clues,
Tales of wonder, everywhere.

Flickering stars like lost dreams,
Painting stories of the night.
As the moonlight softly gleams,
Mysteries weave a mystic sight.

Shadows play in moonlit grace,
Time stands still in quiet awe.
In the heart, a sacred space,
Where the world reveals its flaw.

Step beyond to realms unknown,
Where the fabric of dreams unfold.
Edges blur and seeds are sown,
In enchantment, stories told.

How Spaces Speak

In silence, echoes find their place,
Whispers in the corners trace.
The walls hold stories, soft and clear,
Emotions linger, always near.

Beneath the ceilings, dreams take flight,
Windows frame the morning light.
Each creak, each sigh, a tale they tell,
Of laughter, sorrow, all that fell.

The floors remember fleeting steps,
In gatherings, warmth adept.
A heartbeat resonates with grace,
In every nook, a sacred space.

How spaces speak, in subtle ways,
In moments lost, in softest gaze.
They cradle us through night and day,
In their embrace, we find our way.

Harmony Amongst Halls

Echoes dance along the walls,
In gentle sway, the silence calls.
Each arch and beam, a melody,
Composed in whispers, wild and free.

Footsteps forge a rhythmic path,
In harmony, the echoes laugh.
The heart of space, a vibrant song,
In every hall, we all belong.

With colors bright, the halls unite,
In shadows deep, they find their light.
Together, voices rise and blend,
In this embrace, all hearts transcend.

Harmony reigns where we convene,
In every heartbeat, ever keen.
Amongst the halls, we join the dance,
In unity, we take our chance.

Chronicles of Corners

Corners hold the tales of time,
In quietude, they weave their rhyme.
Where shadows meet, the past resides,
In hidden folds, history abides.

Each crevice forms a whispered plot,
In silence, memories are sought.
With every glance, a story grows,
In corners where the stillness flows.

The crumbling paint, the dust of years,
Bears witness to our hopes and fears.
In corners, life's moments collide,
In a tender space, we confide.

Chronicles penned in softest light,
In corners' grace, we find our sight.
Each whisper, a thread in the seam,
Tales of life, a quiet dream.

Rooted in Rhythm

Beneath the surface, pulse and beat,
In every heart, the rhythms meet.
The ground beneath, a steady thrum,
In roots, the dance of life will come.

With every step, the world aligns,
In syncopation, grace defines.
The trees sway gently, wisdom holds,
In nature's arms, the truth unfolds.

From branches high to soil below,
In silence deep, the feelings flow.
Rooted strongly, yet we soar,
In rhythm found, we yearn for more.

Life's tempo guides, a constant form,
In every heart, we feel the storm.
Rooted in rhythm, we unite,
In harmony, we find our light.

Nestled Narratives

In the crook of ancient trees,
Whispers weave through leaves,
Stories long and softly spun,
Where past and present cleave.

Moonlight dances on the ground,
Casting shadows that confide,
A tapestry of dreams unbound,
In nature's arms, we bide.

Each corner holds a secret voice,
Echoes of forgotten times,
In the hush, we find our choice,
To listen to the rhymes.

Gentle breezes guide us forth,
To places far and wide,
In nestled nooks of mother earth,
The truth we cannot hide.

The Heart's Hideaway

Within the folds of tender care,
A sanctuary we create,
Where trust and love grasp the air,
And worries dissipate.

Soft murmurs linger in the night,
Embracing thoughts, so sweet,
In the glow of candlelight,
Two souls, in silence, meet.

The warmth of laughter fills the space,
Memories softly bloom,
In the heart's hidden embrace,
We find our sacred room.

Every heartbeat tells a tale,
Of journeys shared and dreams,
In this hallowed, timeless vale,
Love's boundless river streams.

Corners That Kiss

Where walls converge with gentle grace,
Two worlds collide and sway,
In quiet corners, time's embrace,
Invites us here to stay.

Sunlight spills like liquid gold,
Revealing paths untold,
In each niche, brave stories unfold,
Rich fabric, bright and bold.

Windows framing life outside,
Offer glimpses fresh and clear,
In the shadows, hearts abide,
Whispers soft, yet near.

Finding peace where moments blend,
In stolen glances found,
These corners, where dreams ascend,
Are sacred, safe, and sound.

Veins of Vitality

Through roots that stretch and intertwine,
Life pulses in a steady flow,
Each leaf a beacon, bold, divine,
In nature's vibrant glow.

Rivers rush with stories bold,
Sharing secrets, wild and free,
In their currents, dreams unfold,
A dance of energy.

Mountains stand with timeless grace,
Guardians of the skies above,
Nature's song, a breathless chase,
Binding all with endless love.

In the heart of every grove,
Lies the essence we embrace,
Veins of vitality, they strove,
Uniting time and space.

Whispers of Sheltered Nooks

In corners where shadows softly play,
Little secrets from the night sway.
Gentle breezes sing their tune,
In the hush of a silvered moon.

Mossy stones hold nature's dreams,
While sunlight through the branches gleams.
Here comfort breathes in every sigh,
As quiet moments softly fly.

Whispers linger in the air,
Stories cherished hide with care.
In sheltered nooks, the heart will find,
A world of peace, forever kind.

Threads of Tranquility

Weave the threads of gentle peace,
In every moment, let worries cease.
Beneath the sky's vast, silent dome,
Find the heartbeat that calls you home.

The river flows with whispered grace,
Carrying dreams to a sacred space.
Among the trees, the silence grows,
Cradling thoughts that softly rose.

A tapestry of light unfolds,
In tranquil patterns, life beholds.
Each thread a chance to start anew,
In the calm embrace, find what's true.

Embracing the Unseen Corners

In unseen corners where shadows hint,
A flicker of hope begins to imprint.
Hidden wonders await each glance,
Inviting the heart to take a chance.

With every turn, a new surprise,
Fragile beauty beneath the skies.
Among the cracks where wildflowers grow,
Life's quiet treasures gently show.

Embrace the whispers that softly call,
In the unheard spaces, we find it all.
Hidden paths lead us to explore,
The magic that waits forevermore.

Echoes of Personalized Sanctuaries

In the stillness, echoes sing,
Of cherished thoughts and simple things.
A sanctuary built from dreams,
Where peace flows in gentle streams.

Each moment carved with tender care,
Familiar scents linger in the air.
Within these walls, a heart takes flight,
Discovering joy in soft twilight.

The touch of memory hangs so fine,
In personalized spaces, love aligns.
Every echo a story to tell,
In the heart's refuge, all is well.

Handwoven Havens

In corners bright where silence sings,
Threads of warmth in soft light cling.
Each knot tied with love's embrace,
Crafting solace, a sacred space.

Beneath the arch of twilight's glow,
Whispers of peace in breezes flow.
Handwoven dreams of lives entwined,
In every stitch, a heart aligned.

Mosaic of Mindful Moments

Fragments of joy, scattered around,
Each piece a story, quietly found.
Colors collide, a gentle blend,
Moments of grace that never end.

In chaos of life, find stillness near,
Hold onto laughter, let go of fear.
Stitching together both light and shade,
Creating a journey beautifully made.

The Art of Place and Purpose

Upon the canvas of earth we tread,
Every step a story, softly said.
We weave our paths with intention clear,
Finding our roots, drawing us near.

In gardens of thought, seeds take flight,
Nurtured by dreams that spark the night.
The art of living in each heartbeat,
Purpose unfolds in moments sweet.

Sculpting Serenity in Shadows

In twilight's embrace, shadows play,
Sculpting peace as night meets day.
With gentle hands, we mold our mind,
Carving out spaces where calm is defined.

Each whisper of dusk brings a chance,
To dance with silence, in a trance.
Finding the beauty in shades we cast,
Serenity sculpted, both present and past.

Canvas of Calm

A blue stretch of the sky,
Waves whispering soft tunes,
Painted sun and clouds drift,
Time holds its gentle breath.

Beneath the leafy trees,
Shadows dance in warm light,
Nature sings a sweet song,
Peace blankets the still earth.

Ripples on the water,
Reflecting dreams of night,
A world wrapped in silence,
Every moment feels right.

In the arms of stillness,
I find solace anew,
The canvas of my heart,
Is brushed with hues of you.

Footprints in the Quiet

Soft whispers on the breeze,
Footsteps traced in the sand,
A path where shadows play,
Nature's gentle command.

With each step I wander,
The world draws me in slow,
Here lies a tranquil peace,
Where only the heart knows.

Footprints leading forward,
Into the still of dawn,
Each print a quiet mark,
Of the journey I've drawn.

In the echo of silence,
Memories softly blend,
In quiet reverie,
I find my soul will mend.

Refuge in the Fray

Amid the stormy chaos,
A quiet heart beats strong,
In the refuge of stillness,
I find where I belong.

Voices rise and tumble,
Like waves upon the shore,
But here, within my spirit,
There's peace forevermore.

The world may rage and spin,
But in this sacred space,
I gather strength around me,
With courage I embrace.

So when the fray surrounds,
And life feels far from fair,
I'll cherish each soft heartbeat,
And breathe in calmness rare.

Arbors of Aspiration

Beneath the spreading boughs,
Dreams whisper on the leaves,
In shadows, light will dance,
Hope breathes and never grieves.

Branches reach for the sky,
Yearning for the bright sun,
Each new sprout tells a tale,
Of battles fought and won.

In the hush of dusk's glow,
Ambitions gently swell,
The arbors stand as witnesses,
To all I dare to tell.

With roots deep in the earth,
And leaves that stretch so high,
I'll climb towards my future,
And watch my dreams take flight.

Landscapes of Lullabies

Gentle hills in twilight glow,
Whispers soft where breezes flow.
Stars emerge, a twinkling hue,
Nighttime sings, dreams born anew.

Waves that cradle sandy shores,
Echoes of forgotten roars.
Moonlight dances on the sea,
Nature's song, a symphony.

Clouds like shadows drift and sway,
Guiding thoughts that float away.
In this peace, the heart finds rest,
In lullabies, we're truly blessed.

Crickets chirp in rhythmic beat,
Nighttime's treasure, pure and sweet.
In the stillness, love arrives,
In these landscapes, hope survives.

Embraces of the Familiar

Familiar streets under soft rain,
Voices echo, joys and pain.
Childhood laughter fills the air,
Comfort found in memories rare.

Porch lights glow, a warm embrace,
Friends gather, share their space.
Stories woven with each glance,
In the light, our spirits dance.

Old trees sway, their branches wide,
Holding secrets, roots that bide.
Sunrise kisses morning dew,
In this space, I cherish you.

Paths we've walked, both near and far,
Guiding us like a shining star.
In every moment, time stands still,
Embraces of love, we all fulfill.

Dwelling of Delicate Dreams

In the quiet, dreams take flight,
Crafting tales that spark the night.
Whispers float on softest sighs,
Dwelling where our hope relies.

Petals fall like secret thoughts,
In this dreamscape, all is caught.
Fragile visions, painted wild,
In the heart of every child.

Gentle breezes coax the stars,
Drawing close our hidden scars.
In these realms, we find our grace,
Every heartbeat, a sacred space.

Through the veil, a light appears,
Guiding us through all our fears.
In this dwelling, spirits gleam,
Crafting worlds from every dream.

Enclaves of Essence

Hidden places, soft and pure,
In these enclaves, hearts endure.
Nature's heartbeat, rhythms blend,
In the quiet, we transcend.

Ancient trees with stories old,
Whisper secrets, brave and bold.
Sunbeams filter through the leaves,
In the stillness, magic weaves.

Rivers run with timeless grace,
Mirroring life's intricate lace.
In this essence, souls align,
Finding peace in every sign.

Here we gather, breathe and hold,
Moments precious, memories gold.
In enclaves deep, we come alive,
In unity, we truly thrive.

Chambers of Creation

In quiet halls where whispers dwell,
Ideas bloom like a secret spell.
Brushes dance on canvas wide,
Imagination's dreams confide.

Echoes linger, shadows blend,
Crafting worlds that never end.
With every stroke, a life unveiled,
In chambers where our hearts have sailed.

From silence comes the vibrant sound,
In art's embrace, we feel profound.
A life of colors, bold and pure,
In every stroke, we seek the cure.

So here we stand, as visions soar,
In chambers vast, we long for more.
To create, to shape, to boldly dream,
In every heart, a radiant gleam.

Textured Tranquility

Softly woven, threads of peace,
A tapestry where tensions cease.
The gentle hum of nature's sigh,
Wraps around as time drifts by.

Leaves whisper tales of ancient trees,
Carried softly by the breeze.
In every fold, a story lies,
Beneath the quilt of endless skies.

Calm reflections on water's face,
Mirror the tranquil, sacred space.
Each layer speaks, a soft embrace,
In textured dreams, we find our place.

So breathe in deep, let worries fade,
In stillness, find the peace we made.
With every thread, a heart's delight,
In tranquility's warm light.

Spirals of Safety

Within our walls, a circle tight,
Holding close through darkest night.
A comforting embrace we find,
In spirals drawn, our hearts entwined.

Waves of calm in swirling grace,
Anchor us in this sacred space.
With every turn, a deeper trust,
In bonds of love, we must adjust.

A refuge built on gentle care,
Where laughter echoes, love is rare.
Together we stand, brave and bold,
In safety's arms, our stories told.

So take my hand, let's spiral in,
Through life's chaos, we'll begin.
In circles dear, forever stay,
In spirals of safety, come what may.

Colors of Contemplation

Brush strokes blend in quiet thought,
A canvas rich with lessons sought.
Each hue a whisper, soft and low,
In colors deep, reflections grow.

Crimson dreams of passion flame,
Azure skies, a heart's reclaimed.
Golden rays of truths unveiled,
In every shade, our fears derailed.

Emerald greens of peace we yearn,
Violet shadows, life's long turn.
In contemplation's gentle maze,
We seek the light in muted haze.

So pause awhile, let colors speak,
In vibrant hues, the strong, the weak.
For in this art of heart's convey,
We find ourselves in shades of gray.

Nooks of Dreams

In corners soft where whispers lie,
The moonlight dances, shadows sigh.
Threads of silk in twilight's glow,
Woven thoughts where dreamers go.

Gentle breezes carry hope,
A tapestry of words and scope.
In every nook, a secret kept,
A universe where starlight crept.

Memories linger, grace the air,
A world unseen, a precious flair.
In quiet moments, the heart can soar,
Through nooks of dreams, forevermore.

Shadows of Sanctuary

Beneath the branches, cool and wide,
Dappled light, where secrets bide.
A sanctuary soft and deep,
In whispered calm, the world can sleep.

Pillowed paths of verdant green,
Shelter found where hearts convene.
Echoes of laughter, soft and low,
In shadows cast, the spirits flow.

Here time dissolves, and worries fade,
In nature's arms, fears are laid.
In shadows of sanctuary, peace will grow,
A tranquil heart where love can glow.

Echoes in the Corners

In quiet rooms where echoes dwell,
Soft whispers weave a timeless spell.
Dust motes dance in golden light,
Memories flutter, taking flight.

Stories linger in every space,
A tapestry of time's embrace.
In corners old, where shadows play,
Echoes hum the past's sweet sway.

Each heartbeat finds a place to rest,
In every nook, a silent quest.
The echoes call, a tender song,
In corners deep, where we belong.

The Art of Nesting

In softest beds of twigs and leaves,
A tapestry of home we weave.
With gentle care, the heart constructs,
A haven safe where love conducts.

Each careful choice, a piece of soul,
Layer by layer, we become whole.
In corners snug, we find our space,
The art of nesting, a warm embrace.

Cradled in comfort, dreams take flight,
As day dissolves into the night.
In every nest, a story springs,
The art of nesting, love it brings.

The Palette of Personal Potency

Colors blend and swirl with grace,
Each hue tells a story, a vivid place.
Shades of courage, strokes of fear,
In this canvas, dreams appear.

Brushes dance in hands so bold,
Painting futures yet untold.
Every mark a step we trace,
In our hearts, we find our space.

A palette rich with golden light,
Mingling shadows, day and night.
Crafting visions, strong and true,
A masterpiece that starts with you.

Meeting Places of Memory

Once shared laughter in the sun,
Echoes linger, memories run.
Footsteps lead to paths we walked,
In silent corners, spirits talked.

Moments shaped like clouds in air,
Fragmented pieces, held with care.
Time a river, winding slow,
In its currents, we all flow.

Faded photographs, whispers soft,
In these spaces, we drift aloft.
Meeting places where souls align,
Building bridges, hearts entwine.

Tapestry of Refuge

Threads of comfort, woven tight,
In darkest hours, a warming light.
Each stitch a promise, gently made,
In this sanctuary, fears will fade.

Patterns of kindness, love's embrace,
In the fabric, find our place.
Colors bright, with stories spun,
Every heart a cherished one.

In the loom of life, we craft,
Binding fragments, tears and laughter.
A tapestry where we belong,
Strength in unity, brave and strong.

Weaving Whispers

Softly spoken, secrets shared,
In the silence, hearts laid bare.
Threads of trust, so finely spun,
Weaving whispers, two become one.

In the shadows, voices blend,
Gentle echoes, never end.
Every word a guiding star,
Illuminating who we are.

A fabric rich with dreams and fears,
Stitched together through the years.
Weaving whispers, night and day,
Creating bonds that never fray.

Resilience in Reconstruction

From ashes we rise, hope in the air,
Brick by brick, mending despair.
Hands in the soil, hearts intertwined,
In every crack, new strength we find.

The storms may rage, the nights be long,
Yet in our hearts, we sing a song.
Together we stand, with dreams in tow,
In resilience, watch our spirits grow.

Each fallen beam, a chance to repair,
With every struggle, we're more aware.
Through trials faced, our spirits ignite,
In the darkness, we bring forth light.

As phoenixes soar from the dust of the past,
We build a future, steadfast and vast.
United in purpose, strong and bold,
Our stories of courage, forever told.

The Space Between

In silence, we linger, a breath held tight,
A world of whispers, beneath the night.
Moments collide, like stars in the sky,
In the space between, our souls learn to fly.

Time drifts slowly, like shadows at dawn,
In gazes exchanged, new beginnings spawn.
We dance on edges, where dreams intertwine,
In that fleeting gap, your hand finds mine.

Between every heartbeat, a longing grows,
In quiet pauses, our true essence shows.
We hold our breath, in a delicate sway,
In the space between, love leads the way.

As echoes fade, and the world turns round,
In the silence shared, our hearts profound.
Between every word, a story unfolds,
In that sacred space, our truth is told.

Inviting Ecstasy in Enclaves

In hidden corners, secrets reside,
Where laughter dances, and spirits collide.
With open hearts, we embrace the night,
Inviting joy, in soft glowing light.

In enclaves of bliss, we weave our tale,
With every heartbeat, we set our sail.
Through valleys of laughter, and peaks of delight,
Together we wander, lost in the night.

The rhythm of life, a seductive embrace,
In every heartbeat, we find our place.
With each whispered dream, our souls take flight,
In inviting ecstasy, hearts feel so right.

As the stars shimmer, and the moon holds sway,
In the cradle of night, we dance and play.
In these moments shared, we boldly proclaim,
In love's sweet enclave, we're never the same.

Relief at the Threshold

At the door of change, a moment's pause,
Breath of fresh air, a silent applause.
Between the known and the vast unknown,
In relief at the threshold, new seeds are sown.

Crossing the line, leaving fears behind,
In the light of hope, our paths aligned.
With every step, we shed the old skin,
In the warmth of the new, let life begin.

The echoes of doubt fade into the past,
In the glow of dawn, freedom comes fast.
A journey awaits, filled with dreams unfurled,
In relief at the threshold, we brave a new world.

Embrace the unknown, let courage ignite,
With hearts wide open, step into the light.
At the door of tomorrow, let joy be your guide,
In relief at the threshold, let your spirit glide.

Blueprints of Belonging

In a world drawn with care,
We sketch the lines of love,
Every stroke a soft embrace,
Every space a heart above.

Foundations built on trust,
Walls adorned with dreams,
Windows wide to the skies,
Echoing laughter's streams.

Paths that lead to warm hearts,
Side by side we roam,
In the blueprint of our lives,
Together we call home.

Tapestry of Touchstone Terrains

Woven threads of sunlight,
Colors blend and sway,
Each strand tells a story,
In this bright array.

Mountains high and valleys low,
Textures rich and vast,
With every touch, we wander,
Through the present and the past.

An embrace of nature's art,
Every path we trace,
In this tapestry we find,
The beauty of our space.

Oases of Imagination

In the desert of our minds,
Dreams bloom like flowers,
Each thought a vibrant hue,
In the shade of quiet hours.

Rivers of creativity,
Flowing soft and free,
An oasis in stillness,
Where all can truly see.

Gather 'round our visions,
Let them dance and play,
In this place of refuge,
We'll chase the night away.

Castles of Comfort

In the heart, we build strong walls,
With love as our base,
Every window wide with joy,
Every corner holds grace.

Turrets reaching high and proud,
Guarding dreams alight,
In the castle of our souls,
We find our peace at night.

The drawbridge lowers gently,
Inviting whispers near,
In this fortress of our making,
Home is ever clear.

Guardians of Inner Landscapes

In shadows deep, the silence breathes,
The guardians stand, their faith deceives.
With whispered thoughts, they guard the light,
In hidden realms, they reign the night.

A tapestry of dreams unfolds,
In secret woods, where time is bold.
They weave the silence, craft the space,
Each heartbeat echoes lost in grace.

With gentle hands, they shape the creeds,
And nurture hope like blooming seeds.
In every corner, wisdom grows,
A symphony where stillness flows.

Through verdant paths, the spirits roam,
In inner realms, they find their home.
These guardians watch, both fierce and kind,
In every heart, their truth aligned.

Curating Comfort Zones

A blanket warm, a cup of tea,
In cozy nooks, we roam so free.
Each corner whispers soft and low,
In comfort's grasp, sweet moments flow.

A chair that cradles weary bones,
A space where love and laughter moans.
With open arms, we share our tales,
In gentle winds, the spirit sails.

Colors warm, the lighting low,
In curated peace, we freely grow.
Each detail crafted with a smile,
To let the heart rest for a while.

In every corner, memories bloom,
In our safe havens, we find room.
Curating joy, a cherished art,
A sacred bond within the heart.

Nestled Narratives

In quiet nooks, the stories dwell,
Nestled tales, a secret spell.
Each whisper holds a moment's thrill,
In memories forged, they linger still.

The attic's dust, the fading light,
Each faded page, a tale takes flight.
In woven words, our past returns,
In gentle fires, the heart still burns.

With every crack, the walls confide,
In cozy spaces, dreams abide.
The tales once told, now softly fade,
In nestled realms, our truths are laid.

From childhood dreams to wisdom's grace,
Each narrative a warm embrace.
Through pages worn, we sail the seas,
In nestled narratives, we find ease.

A Symphony of Surroundings

In morning's light, the world hums sweet,
A symphony of life and heartbeat.
Leaves rustle soft, the birds compose,
In nature's rhythm, beauty flows.

The city's pulse, a vibrant tune,
In bustling streets, the heart's commune.
Each laugh, each sigh, a note of grace,
Together in this shared embrace.

Waves crash loud against the shore,
In ocean's song, we seek for more.
The rustling grass, the whispering trees,
In every sound, the spirit frees.

From quiet dawn to starlit night,
A tapestry of pure delight.
In harmony, our souls align,
In symphony of life, we shine.

Canopies of Comfort

Beneath the leaves, whispers play,
Gentle breezes on warm days.
Nature's arms embrace us tight,
Wrapped in peace, heart takes flight.

Sunlight dances through the trees,
Casting shadows with soft ease.
All the worries fade away,
In this haven, we will stay.

Birds are singing sweet and clear,
In this place, there's naught to fear.
Every branch a story shows,
Underneath, the comfort grows.

Foliage lush and colors bright,
Transforming day into the night.
Here we find our hearts align,
In canopies, we feel divine.

Choreography of Corners

In every turn, a tale unfolds,
Stories penned in bricks of gold.
Footsteps echo, whispers loom,
Choreographed in cozy gloom.

Windows show the world outside,
Yet within, our hearts abide.
Corners cradle souls in rest,
A quiet space where dreams are blessed.

Each angle holds a secret glance,
Inviting us to pause, to dance.
In shadows deep, our hopes ignite,
Choreography wraps us tight.

Home is found in every nook,
Turn the page of life's great book.
In the corners, life's refrain,
Harmonies that soothe the pain.

The Sanctuary We Call Home

Through open doors, peace flows inside,
Where laughter reigns and dreams abide.
Walls enfold us, safe and sound,
In this place, our joys are crowned.

Pictures hang of times long past,
Moments cherished, memories cast.
A warm embrace, a gentle smile,
In our sanctuary, we find style.

The kitchen hums with warmth and cheer,
Shared meals build bonds we hold dear.
Each room tells stories of our own,
In the sanctuary, we have grown.

Together, we weave a thread so fine,
Love and laughter intertwine.
This refuge, where we freely roam,
Forever is our heart's true home.

Spaces Inviting Serenity

In quiet corners, stillness calls,
Soft whispers dance within the walls.
A gentle light warms the air,
Spaces crafted with utmost care.

Cushions piled, a comfy nest,
Here, the heart finds perfect rest.
Tranquil colors, calm and bright,
In these spaces, all feels right.

Windows open to the breeze,
Nature's sigh brings sweet unease.
A moment's pause, the mind unwinds,
In serenity, true peace finds.

Every corner, a soft embrace,
In these spaces, we trace grace.
Gathered moments, quiet and clear,
Inviting serenity, drawing near.

The Alchemy of Ambiance

In whispers of dusk, the light softly fades,
Colors blend gently, the atmosphere sways.
Shadows and echoes dance in the night,
Each moment a spell, a fragile delight.

Candles flicker bright, warmth fills the air,
Textures entwined in a subtle affair.
Music lingers lightly, a soft serenade,
Crafting a space where memories are made.

Nature's soft sigh mingles with laughter,
Moments like jewels, strung together after.
Every corner alive, a story to tell,
The magic of ambiance casting its spell.

In this alchemy sweet, we find our retreat,
Creating a haven where heart and home meet.
With each breath we take, the ambiance grows,
An artful embrace, as the evening glows.

Pathways to Peace

Gentle winds whisper through the tall trees,
A tranquil symphony, nature's soft tease.
Step by step forward, let worries unwind,
In this sacred space, serenity's blind.

Rivers of stillness flow through my mind,
Each ripple a promise, the soul's peace defined.
Paths carved in silence, soft earth 'neath my feet,
A journey of calm, where heartbeats repeat.

The sun dips below, painting skies with grace,
Golden horizons, a warm embrace.
In every exhale, let tensions release,
Finding within me the essence of peace.

With nature as guide, I wander and roam,
Each step a heartbeat, this Earth is my home.
In pathways of peace, I discover my way,
A sanctuary found, come what may.

Elements of Expressive Environments

Colors that pulse, alive like a dream,
Textures that whisper, an artist's theme.
Each corner a canvas, a tale to unfold,
A symphony spoken in hues bright and bold.

Light dances through windows, casting bright graces,
Filling each space with warmth and embraces.
The air resonates with laughter and sound,
In expressive environments, joy is profound.

Shapes intertwine in a playful embrace,
Inviting the mind to explore and chase.
Every surface a canvas, a playground of art,
Expressive elements sing to the heart.

In gatherings shared, we shape our surrounds,
Creating a tapestry, magic abounds.
Through art and intention, we carve out a glow,
Elements of life, vibrant and aglow.

Beyond Four Walls

Step outside the doors, let the wild air flow,
Beyond four walls, the wonders will grow.
Nature invites us to breathe and explore,
With each step we take, we find so much more.

Mountains stand tall, guardians of dreams,
Rivers unspooling, with laughter and seams.
Fields stretch for miles, a canvas so wide,
In this realm of freedom, we wander with pride.

Sky becomes endless, a palette of stars,
Where night sings sweet lullabies from afar.
Each moment is fleeting, yet joyfully shines,
Beyond four walls, our spirit aligns.

Connections with nature, a tapestry spun,
With every new dawn, a new life begun.
Embrace the adventure, let your heart sway,
Beyond four walls, we find our own way.

Traces of Touch

Fingers brush in soft twilight,
A whisper lost, a fleeting sight.
Memories linger, shadows play,
In the silence, they softly stay.

Warmth left on a scarlet thread,
Words unspoken, a bond unsaid.
In the space where pulses blend,
Every touch marks how hearts mend.

Echoes of laughter, light and free,
In the echoes, a tranquil plea.
Gentle moments, like soft rain,
Imprints left that ease the pain.

In the twilight, we find our way,
With each trace, we learn to stay.
In the dance of time, we flow,
Finding home in what we know.

Heartbeats in Empty Rooms

Walls hold stories, breaths inside,
Faint echoes where whispers bide.
Each heartbeat marks a secret time,
In these corners, silence climbs.

Shadows dance on walls so bare,
Memories linger, fill the air.
In the stillness, a pulse of grace,
Echoes of life in this empty space.

Footsteps falter, then retreat,
In the quiet, we find our beat.
Each thud a reminder, love entwined,
In the hush, our souls aligned.

Stillness surrounds like a soft quilt,
In these chambers, hope is built.
Heartbeats thrum, a steady tune,
In the night, beneath the moon.

Vignettes of Vitality

Life's bright strokes on canvas gray,
Each moment, a vivid display.
Colors burst in joyful sway,
In these vignettes, dreams hold sway.

Sunrise paints the world anew,
With each dawn, we chase what's true.
Petals dance in gentle breeze,
In their flutter, hearts find ease.

Raindrops echo on windowpanes,
Nature's song, all joy remains.
In small gestures, love ignites,
Creating warmth on chilly nights.

Every heartbeat, a vibrant call,
In every rise, we softly fall.
Life's mosaic, pieced with care,
Vignettes linger, everywhere.

Quadrants of Quietude

In the corners, stillness thrives,
Softly wrapped in muted lives.
Shadows gather, gentle grace,
Within these walls, our thoughts embrace.

Time flows slowly, like a stream,
In the hush, we weave a dream.
Moments blend, like colors mixed,
In quietude, life's canvas fixed.

A sigh escapes, the only sound,
In tranquility, peace is found.
Words unspoken, feelings share,
In silence, we breathe the air.

As daylight dims, stars peep through,
In their glow, our spirits renew.
In these quadrants, calm and bright,
We find solace in the night.

Milton Keynes UK
Ingram Content Group UK Ltd.
UKHW020048181024
449757UK00011B/572